I0820958

NORTH AMERICAN FIELD GUIDES

# WATERFOWL

Carol Hand

Field Guides

An Imprint of Abdo Reference | abdobooks.com

# CONTENTS

Dabbling Ducks
Diving Ducks
Sea Ducks
Geese
Swans

# WHAT ARE WATERFOWL?

Waterfowl belong to the order Anseriformes and the family Anatidae, which includes ducks, geese, and swans. Waterfowl are medium to large birds that live on or near water. Most prefer freshwater habitats, including lakes, ponds, and freshwater beaches. Waterfowl usually feed on water plants. Some also eat insects, mollusks, and other aquatic invertebrates.

About 160 species of ducks, geese, and swans are found around the world on all continents except Antarctica. Many waterfowl species are native to North America, but some were introduced from other places. At least 36 species of ducks, seven species of geese, and three species of swans live in North America. Most of these are native. A few were introduced from other places and now live on the continent. Two of the most common North American waterfowl are the mallard duck and the Canada goose.

## WATERFOWL CHARACTERISTICS

Waterfowl have plump bodies that are either egg shaped or tapered at both ends. They have short, sturdy legs and webbed feet, making them excellent swimmers. Their bills are broad and usually flattened. These birds have short, pointed wings and strong pectoral muscles that make them powerful fliers.

Waterfowl have watertight plumage. Their fluffy down feathers keep them warm. The outer feathers are smooth and overlapping, causing water to bead up and roll off. This keeps the down feathers dry. Waterfowl also have preen glands. A preen gland is an oil gland at the base of the tail. The birds spread oil on their feathers to make them even more waterproof.

# WATERFOWL IDENTIFICATION

Most waterfowl are ducks, which are separated into three groups: dabbling ducks, diving ducks, and sea ducks. Dabbling ducks, or dabblers, feed in shallow water and rarely go below the surface. They feed at the surface or tip their rear ends up, feeding on underwater plants. Dabblers forage, or look for food, both on land and in water. To fly, they take off directly from the water.

Diving ducks, or divers, live and feed in deeper water. They find food by diving and swimming underwater. They walk awkwardly on land. To fly, divers take off by running across the water's surface.

Sea ducks spend most of their time in or near coastal waters. Many diving ducks are also sea ducks. Members of this group of ducks have salt glands that remove salt from their bodies. This lets the ducks drink salt water. They breed in the far north, including Alaska and northern Canada, and are adapted to living in frigid waters.

Aside from ducks, geese and swans are also waterfowl. Geese are larger than ducks. They have shorter bills. Swans are similar to geese, but they are even larger with longer necks and greater wingspans.

There are some characteristics people can look for when identifying waterfowl:

- Size: The wingspan and body weight
- North American Range: The regions where the waterfowl is found in North America
- Habitat: The places where the waterfowl can be found, such as ponds or the ocean
- Diet: What kinds of foods the waterfowl eats

# DEEP DIVE ON WATERFOWL

Waterfowl come in many sizes. The smallest waterfowl species in North America is the green-winged teal at 0.2 to 1.1 pounds (0.1 to 0.5 kg). The largest, the trumpeter swan, is one of the heaviest flying birds in the world at up to 29 pounds (13 kg).

Many waterfowl are shades of black, gray, brown, and white, although some are brightly colored. Individual birds may change color throughout the year. During the breeding season, male ducks are often more colorful than females. Male and female geese and swans, while similar in color, can vary in size. All waterfowl have relatively long necks when compared to most other birds. Ducks' necks are the shortest of the waterfowl.

## ANNUAL CYCLES

Waterfowl life involves four annual activities. These are breeding, molting, migration, and wintering. Breeding includes egg incubation and raising of young. In North America, breeding often occurs in the far north.

**The male, *left*, and female, *right*, wood ducks look different from each other.**

Common eiders lay four to five eggs.

Most ducks are seasonally monogamous. That means they form pair bonds for a single breeding season. Female ducks usually care for ducklings on their own. Males may help build nests and stay to protect the females during egg laying. But once incubation begins, the males leave.

Ducks carry out complex courtship rituals to form pair bonds, including vocalizations and dance-like movements. The female chooses her mate based on the male's plumage as well as his display. Each species has courtship display moves that they perform by instinct.

The male common goldeneye's courtship display involves tilting its head back and then thrusting it up.

## DEEP DIVE ON WATERFOWL

Swans and many geese are monogamous, forming pairs for life. They form pair bonds after the age of one year. Geese first lay and incubate eggs during their second year or later. Swans do not lay eggs until year four. In geese and swans, both males and females raise the young.

North American waterfowl usually nest on the ground near water. Nests are made of plant materials and down feathers. Wood ducks and a few other species nest in holes in trees. Females lay a clutch, or batch, of between 2 and 13 eggs. Waterfowl incubate their eggs for 21 to 31 days, depending on the species. Baby ducks are called ducklings. Baby geese are goslings, and baby swans are cygnets.

**A Canada goose nest can be made of grasses, mosses, other plant materials, and feathers.**

**When molting after breeding, male ducks lose their brightly colored breeding feathers, which are replaced with duller camouflaged colors.**

Between the breeding season and migration, all waterfowl molt. Both flight and down feathers wear out and must be replaced. Many birds lose all their flight feathers at once. Flight feathers are the stiff feathers on the wings and tail that help with flight. The birds grow new flight feathers in place of the lost ones. During this several-week period, the birds are unable to fly. The molting process begins just after the eggs hatch, usually in mid-May, and lasts through July.

After the breeding season, waterfowl migrate to the southern United States, Mexico, or Central America. Migrations, depending on the species, can be either short or thousands of miles long. Groups of different species often remain near each other, feeding and migrating together.

**Waterfowl usually migrate in groups.**

Mallard ducklings hatch with yellow and brown feathers.

Wintering is the final stage of the cycle. The birds stay in warm southern areas over winter. They rest in regions with high food supplies, feeding to regain the fat stores they used up during migration. When spring comes, the birds migrate north again for breeding.

## YOUNG WATERFOWL

All young waterfowl hatch covered in down feathers. Waterfowl young are able to eat and swim on their own almost immediately after birth. They can see, walk, and follow their parents.

Ducklings

Within 24 to 48 hours after hatching, the mother duck leads her hatchlings to a wetland, where they begin feeding on their own. The first two weeks after hatching are dangerous for ducklings. They protect themselves by hiding, using the camouflage of their down feathers and surrounding vegetation. The mother keeps them warm with her wings and body, finds hiding places, and distracts predators.

In the third through sixth weeks of life, ducklings lose their down and begin to grow flight feathers. By seven to eight weeks of age, they are almost fully grown. They have eclipse plumage, which has dull, camouflaged colors like adult female plumage. They begin to make longer flights and prepare for their first migration.

The first days and weeks of life for goslings and cygnets are similar. Both parents remain with the goslings. For the first week, an adult goose continues to keep them safe and warm by sitting on them. Goslings are covered in yellowish down. They are much larger than ducklings and leave the nest within 24 hours of hatching.

Gosling

Goslings begin to molt at 20 days to one month. They appear fluffy and patchy for about three to six weeks as their first juvenile feathers appear, which happens between four and eight weeks of age. At this time, they fledge, or take their first flight. They get their adult plumage at about 1.5 years old.

Cygnet

Cygnets have grayish down. They turn all white after a year. Juveniles have pink bills with black tips. The bills turn all black during the birds' first winter. They swim within a day or two of hatching. Cygnets often ride on their parents' backs for the first two weeks after hatching.

Young swans are fully feathered by nine to ten weeks of age and begin to make short flights at 14 to 15 weeks old. They migrate with their parents to wintering areas, spend the winter, and then migrate north with their parents. When they are about one year old, the parents drive them away, and they form their own families.

## WATERFOWL ECOLOGY

To survive and thrive, waterfowl require healthy wetland habitats, such as marshes. One of the best waterfowl habitats is the prairie pothole region of the Midwest, which has many small, seasonally flooding wetlands. However, human development in these areas has caused many of these habitats to be drained and lost.

**Young waterfowl, including goslings, look scruffy when molting.**

The movement of waterfowl through wetlands is key to the transport of nutrients and organisms within these habitats. As they move from one wetland to another, waterfowl carry plant seeds and aquatic invertebrates. This helps maintain wetland biodiversity.

Waterfowl have many predators, both on land and in water. Mammals that prey on waterfowl include red foxes, striped skunks, raccoons, and coyotes. Bird predators include crows, magpies, hawks, and owls. Humans are a major waterfowl predator. Most species of waterfowl are hunted as game birds.

**The prairie pothole region is concentrated in North Dakota, South Dakota, Minnesota, and Wisconsin.**

## WATERFOWL HUNTING

People have hunted waterfowl for food and feathers for thousands of years. Since 1500, seven species of the family Anatidae have gone extinct due to human hunting. Waterfowl are still threatened by hunting and other factors, including pollution, habitat loss, and invasive species. However, according to the US Fish and Wildlife Service, waterfowl populations have slightly increased since the 1970s.

Waterfowl hunting occurs across the country but is concentrated along the four flyways. Flyways are routes that connect waterfowl breeding and wintering grounds. These pathways are thousands of miles long and provide stopping places where migrating birds can rest and feed. North America has four major flyways. These are the Pacific, Central, Mississippi, and Atlantic Flyways.

Councils representing each flyway help monitor waterfowl populations and conserve their habitats. The birds live along these major migratory pathways year-round. But they are present in the largest numbers during the spring and fall migrations.

**Hunters often use trained dogs such as Labrador retrievers to find downed waterfowl and bring them back to the hunters.**

The US government enforces rules about the species and numbers of birds that can be killed in the United States. Because waterfowl are migratory, their populations move across many states, so the federal government manages their conservation. One federal requirement is that any hunter over 16 years old must buy a Federal Duck Stamp to legally hunt waterfowl. Most of the stamp's purchase price is used for the government to buy wetland habitat.

Several organizations help waterfowl hunters. Some assist with the duck-hunting experience. This includes selecting hunting locations, creating custom schedules, planning travel, and securing hunting licenses. Hunters may use these agencies so they can just relax and enjoy a hunting trip.

**Large numbers of waterfowl gather briefly at lakes and ponds along the flyways when migrating.**

Conserving wetlands helps ducks survive and thrive.

## WATERFOWL CONSERVATION

Ducks Unlimited (DU) is a nonprofit organization focused on the conservation of North American waterfowl habitats. DU conserves, restores, and manages wetlands, benefiting not only waterfowl but also people and ecosystems. In 2024, DU was responsible for the conservation of more than 1,560 square miles (4,040 sq km) of waterfowl habitat. Since its formation in the 1930s, it has conserved about 29,690 square miles (76,900 sq km) of grasslands and wetlands in Canada, the United States, and Mexico.

STEPTOE VALLEY WMA

THIS WETLAND ENHANCEMENT PROJECT LOCATED WITHIN THE MEADOW NORTH OF THIS SIGN WAS ACCOMPLISHED THROUGH THE COOPERATIVE EFFORTS OF A DIVERSE PARTNERSHIP INCLUDING: NEVADA WATERFOWL ASSOCIATION, BARRICK GOLDSTRIKE MINES, WHITE PINE COUNTY SPORTSMAN'S ASSOCIATION, TROUT UNLIMITED, THE FAIRWEATHER FOUNDATION, GREAT BASIN BIRD OBSERVATORY, NEVADA STATE LANDS, WILDLIFE AND HABITAT IMPROVEMENT IN NEVADA AND THOSE REPRESENTED BELOW. THIS PROJECT WILL PROVIDE QUALITY HABITAT FOR AN ARRAY OF WETLAND DEPENDENT SPECIES AND A QUALITY RECREATIONAL EXPERIENCE FOR USERS OF THE AREA.

Ducks Unlimited sometimes partners with other organizations to conserve wetlands.

**Banded duck**

DU's membership is composed of duck hunters, conservationists, and outdoor enthusiasts. Its primary goal in conserving habitats is to ensure a steady supply of ducks for hunting. In the process, it improves and increases waterfowl habitat by repairing and restoring damaged wetlands, planting vegetation, and helping scientists and engineers bring drained marshes back to life. It also purchases existing wetlands and passes them on to conservationists for long-term management.

Since the 1950s, waterfowl populations have been closely monitored through yearly population surveys, banding, and information provided by hunters. Banding is when researchers place a numbered band around a bird's leg to help keep track of the population. Also, many groups work internationally to conserve waterfowl habitat.

The US Congress passed the North American Wetlands Conservation Act (NAWCA) in 1989. In addition to conserving waterfowl populations and habitat, the NAWCA has programs to decrease coastal erosion, control flooding, and refill groundwater supplies. Since the 1990s, the act has benefited about 48,440 square miles (125,500 sq km) of habitat.

# HOW TO USE THIS BOOK

**Tab shows the waterfowl category.**

DIVING DUCKS

## REDHEAD *(AYTHYA AMERICANA)*

Redheads are slightly smaller than canvasbacks, with
rounded heads and steep foreheads. Male redheads have
black breasts and tails, and light
ow. Females' bodies are light
th males and females have

**The waterfowl's common name appears here.**

Female, *left*, and male, *right*

### NEST PARASITISM

Some waterfowl species lay their eggs in the nests of
other females of the same or different species. The foster
mothers raise the ducklings as their own. This strategy
is known as nest parasitism or egg dumping. Waterfowl
known to do this include redheads, canvasbacks, wood
ducks, hooded mergansers, and snow geese.
more than 90 percent of canvasback nests
lhead eggs.

66

**Sidebars provide additional information about the topic.**

The waterfowl's scientific name appears here.

## HOW TO SPOT

**Size:** Wingspan 30 to 31 inches (75 to 79 cm); 1.3 to 3.3 pounds (0.6 to 1.5 kg)

**North American Range:** Central Alaska, southern Canada, and the United States to Guatemala and the Caribbean

**Habitat:** Wetlands, especially Midwestern prairie potholes; the Great Lakes; the Gulf Coast; and other coastlines

**Diet:** Submerged aquatic plants and animals including algae, bulrush, pondweed, widgeon grass, fish eggs, snails, zebra mussels, and aquatic insects

Male

*How to Spot* boxes give information about the waterfowl's size, range, habitat, and diet.

Female with ducklings

Images show the waterfowl.

Redheads and canvasbacks are often found together during both the breeding and wintering seasons. Outside the breeding season, redheads gather in huge rafts on the water, often mixing with canvasbacks, scaups, wigeons, and coots. They dive in shallower water than most diving ducks and often get food in the same way as dabbling ducks, by tipping up in the water. Redheads practice nest parasitism.

67

These paragraphs give information about the waterfowl.

# AMERICAN BLACK DUCK

## *(ANAS RUBRIPES)*

The American black duck is large, similar in size and shape to the closely related mallard. It is dark with a chocolate-colored body, pale grayish-brown head, and yellowish-green bill. Females are slightly lighter in color than males. Both sexes have bright blue wing patches and white underwings. The American black duck often breeds with the mallard. The hybrid offspring usually have some mallard features.

Male

### HOW TO SPOT

**Size:** Wingspan 35 to 37 inches (88 to 95 cm); 1.5 to 3.5 pounds (0.7 to 1.6 kg)

**North American Range:** Central and eastern Canada to Florida in the United States

**Habitat:** Wetlands in freshwater and salt marshes; protected ponds, marshes, and bays

**Diet:** Aquatic plants, invertebrates, small fish, and grain

Male

This duck is common in the northeastern United States and Canada. Although common, American black ducks are shy. They are better adapted to woods than to open lands, and populations have fallen as wooded habitat has declined. They winter farther north than most dabbling ducks and are well adapted to living in tidewater areas.

Ducklings

**FUN FACT**
Many ducks, such as American black ducks, have stripes across their shiny eyes. This camouflage helps them hide from predators.

Female

# AMERICAN WIGEON

## *(MARECA AMERICANA)*

The male American wigeon has a brown body, a bright white blaze on the forehead, and a bright green slash behind the eye. The male is a richer brown than the female. Both have white underwings. On the water, they often keep their heads down, so they appear to have no necks. The white patch on the forehead has earned them the nickname "baldpates." *Pate* is another word for head.

**FUN FACT**

**American wigeons' North American populations declined by about 56 percent from 1966 through 2019, though they are still relatively common ducks.**

Female

Male

## HOW TO SPOT

**Size:** Average wingspan 33 inches (84 cm); 1.1 to 2.9 pounds (0.5 to 1.3 kg)

**North American Range:** Throughout Canada, the United States, and Mexico; parts of Central America and the Caribbean

**Habitat:** Ponds, lakes, wetlands, bays, estuaries, and agricultural fields

**Diet:** Aquatic plants such as widgeon grass, cattail, sedge, and duckweed; terrestrial plants such as grass, clover, rice, wheat, and barley

Although defined as dabbling ducks, American wigeons feed both on land and in deep water. They eat more plants than other dabbling ducks. This duck's short, goose-like bill is well adapted for pulling vegetation from fields. While in deep water, the American wigeon steals food from diving ducks and coots.

The American wigeon breeds in Alaska and the northern Canadian provinces. During courtship displays, males give high-pitched whistles. Males begin the fall migration before females and juveniles. On wintering grounds, they congregate with other species, including mallards, gadwalls, and coots.

# BLACK-BELLIED WHISTLING DUCK *(DENDROCYGNA AUTUMNALIS)*

The black-bellied whistling duck is named for its black belly and whistling call. It has a long neck, bright pink legs, and a bright pink or orange bill. Its body is mostly chestnut red. It has a chestnut cap of feathers on its head.

## HOW TO SPOT

**Size:** Wingspan 34 to 37 inches (86 to 95 cm); 1.5 to 2.2 pounds (0.7 to 1 kg)

**North American Range:** Southern United States to Central America

**Habitat:** Edges of shallow ponds, lawns, golf courses, schoolyards, and agricultural fields, especially flooded rice fields

**Diet:** Grain; plants such as smartweed, marsh grasses, and sedges; and small aquatic animals such as snails, insects, and spiders

Black-bellied whistling ducks have several characteristics that are unusual for ducks. They are one of the few duck species that nest and perch in trees. They readily use artificial nest boxes. Males and females are similar in size and color. Unlike most ducks, they form long-term pair bonds. In this way, they are more like geese and swans.

This duck flocks to agricultural fields both day and night to forage on seeds and grains. It can dabble in shallow water or reach underwater for emergent plants. Females often lay eggs in group nests. Known as dump nests, these can contain 60 or more eggs. Both parents incubate the eggs, another unusual behavior for a duck.

**FUN FACT**

**Ducks and geese control their feathers using 12,000 or more skin muscles. These muscles help them dive, regulate body heat, and express emotions such as aggression and attraction to mates.**

Duckling

# BLUE-WINGED TEAL

## *(SPATULA DISCORS)*

Blue-winged teals are very small dabbling ducks. They are the second most common ducks after mallards. Most of the male teal's body is buffy, a dull yellowish brown, with black speckles. The bill, wings, and rear are black with a white patch just before the rear. The head is slate blue with a pure white crescent behind the bill. Females and immature males are buffy brown all over. In flight, both males and females display powder-blue patches on their upper wing feathers.

Female

Male

**FUN FACT**

**The blue-winged teal migrates farther than any other North American waterfowl. Its longest known migration is 4,000 miles (6,400 km) between Oak Lake, Manitoba, and Lima, Peru.**

## HOW TO SPOT

**Size:** Wingspan 22 to 24 inches (56 to 62 cm); 0.4 to 1.1 pounds (0.2 to 0.5 kg)

**North American Range:** Alaska and Canada through Panama

**Habitat:** Calm waters, including small lakes, marshes, and prairie potholes; grassland habitats mixed with wetlands; and around the edges of ponds

**Diet:** Vegetation, grain, and aquatic insects such as midge larvae; crustaceans, clams, and snails

Ducklings

Male

Blue-winged teals are warm-weather ducks. They winter in South America, migrating north late in spring and south early in fall. They are fast fliers and migrate long distances over the open ocean. Flocks moving south in the fall sometimes contain only young teals. This suggests migration routes are instinctive rather than learned. This species is seasonally monogamous.

# CINNAMON TEAL

## *(SPATULA CYANOPTERA)*

There are five subspecies of cinnamon teals in the Western Hemisphere. One, the northern cinnamon teal, lives in western North America. The other four live in South America.

The cinnamon teal is a small duck with a relatively large head and long black bill. The breeding male has a rusty reddish-brown body during breeding season with a black back and rear. It has red eyes. Females and nonbreeding males have brown bodies and heads. All adults have large sky-blue patches on the wings, which are visible in flight. Females are often mistaken for blue-winged teals.

### HOW TO SPOT

**Size:** Wingspan 21 to 22 inches (54 to 57 cm); 0.7 to 0.9 pounds (0.3 to 0.4 kg)

**North American Range:** Southwestern Canada and western United States into Guatemala

**Habitat:** Freshwater wetlands, streams, reservoirs, ponds, and ditches

**Diet:** Seeds and shoots of marsh grasses such as bulrushes, smartweed, pondweed, and millet; some invertebrates such as snails, beetles, midges, and dragonflies

**Male, *left*, and female, *right***

Cinnamon teals feed, breed, and molt in marshes. When feeding, they swim slowly in large groups, almost in unison. Cinnamon teals are generally monogamous during breeding season. They have complex, ritualized mating displays, with many males often performing for a single female. The male protects his mate and defends a small territory during nest-building and incubation.

# FULVOUS WHISTLING DUCK

## *(DENDROCYGNA BICOLOR)*

The fulvous whistling duck is mallard sized but has a longer neck and legs, giving it a lanky appearance. Its head and body are a rich rusty cinnamon color, and it has broad black stripes across the back and wings. The tail is black, and the undertail is white. The duck's sides have white stripes, and the bill and legs are dark bluish gray. The sexes look similar.

The fulvous whistling duck has a whistling call. The species is highly social, and after breeding season these ducks gather in large flocks with other species. In fulvous whistling ducks, a pair bond lasts for several years. Both parents incubate the eggs, and the male helps protect the young.

**FUN FACT**

**Some fulvous whistling ducks migrate in seemingly random directions, at times flying hundreds of miles north to winter in places such as Canada.**

## HOW TO SPOT

**Size:** Wingspan 33 to 37 inches (85 to 93 cm); 1.1 to 2.2 pounds (0.5 to 1 kg)

**North American Range:** Texas, Louisiana, Florida, Mexico, and the Caribbean

**Habitat:** Freshwater marshes, rice fields, crayfish farms, and flooded pastures

**Diet:** Invertebrates such as earthworms, midges, aquatic insects, snails, and small mollusks; seeds of rice, wheat, grasses, and sedges

Ducklings

Populations of fulvous whistling ducks are at risk in some places because they depend on rice fields and other flooded crops. This exposes them to pesticides and hunting. Loss of their marsh habitats is also a problem. However, US populations were increasing in the early 2020s.

# GADWALL *(MARECA STREPERA)*

Gadwalls are slightly smaller than mallards, and they have thinner, darker bills. Males and females look similar, both resembling female mallards. They are sometimes called gray ducks, and their silver-gray plumage has curvy patterns. During breeding season, the male's head is brownish, and the tail feathers are black. Female plumage is similar, but the back is more brownish and the breast more buffy tan. Both sexes display white wing patches during flight.

## HOW TO SPOT

**Size:** Wingspan 33 inches (84 cm); 1.1 to 2.9 pounds (0.5 to 1.3 kg)

**North American Range:** Southern Alaska, southern Canada, and throughout the United States and Mexico

**Habitat:** Plains, prairies, reservoirs, ponds, marshes, city parks, sewage ponds, and edges of estuaries

**Diet:** Aquatic vegetation such as algae, grasses, rushes, and pondweed; invertebrates such as snails, midges, and water beetles

Male

Gadwalls tend to feed deeper than other dabbling ducks. They do not dive but rather tip forward and stretch their necks to feed on submerged vegetation. They also steal food from diving ducks and coots.

They form pairs during fall migration, earlier than most ducks. However, they breed later than most species. Nests are made in dense grass or brush within 200 yards (180 m) of water. The ducks may nest on islands for greater protection from predators. Gadwalls are widespread and adaptable. Their numbers have risen since the 1980s.

Duckling

Male, *left*, and female, *right*

## PAIR BONDING

Each duck species has unique displays for pair bonding. A male gadwall seeks a female's attention by ruffling his head feathers, drawing his head close to his body and then pushing it forward as he rears out of the water. Groups of male cinnamon teals perform ritualized preening, head motions, and other displays while a single female watches. The female swims in front of her chosen male. Groups of male mallards display by shaking their heads and tails, bobbing their heads, dipping, and whistling.

# GREEN-WINGED TEAL

## *(ANAS CRECCA)*

Green-winged teals are North America's smallest dabbling ducks. They have short bills and short necks. The male's head is cinnamon colored with a wide, bright green streak running from both eyes to the back of the neck. The female is brown and has a buffy yellow streak along the tail. Both sexes have green wing patches that are visible during flight.

Female

Ducklings

## LAMELLAE

A duck's bill is lined with many closely packed, comb-like structures called lamellae. The word *lamellae* comes from a Latin word meaning "thin plates." Although they look like teeth, lamellae are not used to chew. Instead, they act as filters, letting water and mud drain out while keeping bits of edible plant and animal matter trapped in the bill.

## HOW TO SPOT

**Size:** Wingspan 20 to 23 inches (52 to 59 cm); 0.2 to 1.1 pounds (0.1 to 0.5 kg)

**North American Range:**
Alaska and Canada to the United States, Mexico, and the Caribbean

**Habitat:** River deltas, wetlands, prairie potholes, beaver ponds, lakes, grasslands, and meadows

**Diet:** Mostly aquatic invertebrates and seeds

Feeding green-winged teals may tip up in shallow water to feed on submerged vegetation or pick up pieces of food while standing in shallow water. They occasionally dive for food or to avoid predators. They use the comb-like lamellae around the edges of their bills to filter small invertebrates from the water.

Males attract females with elaborate mating displays, including movements and vocalizations. Up to 25 males gather together to court females in flight and on the water. The male defends the female during breeding but leaves once incubation begins.

# MALLARD *(ANAS PLATYRHYNCHOS)*

Mallards are the most common ducks and the ancestors of almost all domestic ducks. They are among the largest ducks, with long, sturdy bodies. Males have iridescent-green heads with narrow white bands on their necks and broad, flat, yellow bills. Their bodies are gray, their wings and breasts are brown, and their rears are black. Female and juvenile plumage is mottled brown, and their bills are orange and brown. Both sexes have blue wing patches with white borders visible during flight.

Male, *left*, female, *middle*, and duckling, *right*

## HOW TO SPOT

**Size:** Wingspan 32 to 37 inches (82 to 95 cm); 2.2 to 2.9 pounds (1 to 1.3 kg)

**North American Range:** Alaska, Canada, southern Greenland, the United States, Mexico, and the Caribbean

**Habitat:** All types of wetlands, including ponds, lakes, rivers, marshes, and coastal habitats; parks and suburban yards

**Diet:** Seeds, grains, and aquatic vegetation; animal matter such as aquatic insect larvae, earthworms, snails, and freshwater shrimp

Mallards have one of the largest breeding ranges of any North American duck, covering Canada and the northern third of the United States. They winter throughout the United States but especially along the Mississippi Flyway. They live alongside other species of dabbling ducks and can breed with some of them.

Male

**FUN FACT**

The quack, which has come to symbolize the sound of a duck, is the voice of the female mallard. Most ducks do not quack. The male mallard makes a raspy call. Other species whistle, peep, grunt, or groan.

Duckling

# MEXICAN DUCK *(ANAS DIAZI)*

The Mexican duck, once considered a subspecies of the mallard, is now seen as a separate species. It resembles the female mallard but is slightly smaller and darker. The male has cinnamon-colored highlights, and the female has buffy highlights. The male's bill is yellow, and the female's is orange and black. In flight, both sexes display white underwings. In the southwestern United States, Mexican ducks sometime breed with mallards. The offspring have coloring between the two species.

Female

Males

**FUN FACT**

Mexican ducks appear to be expanding their range northward. In the spring and summer of 2019, a birder found several Mexican ducks in the mountains of Colorado.

Male Mexican duck–mallard hybrid

## HOW TO SPOT

**Size:** Wingspan unavailable; 1.8 to 2.6 pounds (0.8 to 1.2 kg)

**North American Range:** Arizona, New Mexico, Texas, and Mexico

**Habitat:** Arid and semiarid areas and almost all aquatic habitats, including permanent lakes, rivers, streams, ponds, marshes, and intermittent streams

**Diet:** Wheat, barley, oats, garbanzo beans, seeds of aquatic plants, weeds, plant tubers, and invertebrates

Male Mexican duck–mallard hybrid

About 98 percent of Mexican ducks live and breed in Mexico, southwestern Texas, and southern Arizona and New Mexico. Mexican ducks breed during the rainy season, from June through October. They form large flocks during the dry season. The species has relatively low numbers and a limited range, but its population is stable.

# MOTTLED DUCK *(ANAS FULVIGULA)*

In appearance, mottled ducks are halfway between female mallards and American black ducks. They are similar in size and shape to mallards, having short necks and tails and large bills. The bodies of both sexes are deep brown with buff streaks. Their faces and necks are solid buff. The tail is dark. If the tail has white, the bird is probably a mallard hybrid. The male's bill is bright yellow with a black tip. The female's bill is greenish yellow to orange and can have dark markings.

## HOW TO SPOT

**Size:** Wingspan 31 to 34 inches (80 to 87 cm); 1.5 to 2.6 pounds (0.7 to 1.2 kg)

**North American Range:** US and Mexican Gulf Coast and throughout Florida

**Habitat:** Freshwater wetlands including marshes, lakes, and ponds; flooded fields; stormwater collection areas; and sewage treatment plants

**Diet:** Plant matter including seeds and shoots of grasses, millet, smartweed, spike rush, bulrush, and cultivated rice; animal matter including snails, crayfish, beetles, dragonflies, and small fish

Adult with ducklings

There are two nonmigratory populations of mottled ducks. One is in Florida, and the other is along the western Gulf Coast. The latter population has decreased by about half since the early 2000s. Causes of declines in both populations may include poor reproductive success, increasing droughts, and hybridization with mallards, especially in Florida.

Female, *left*, and male, *right*

## HYBRIDIZATION IN DUCKS

Hybridization occurs when ducks of two different species breed and produce offspring. In Florida, mallards and mottled ducks are hybridizing, producing so-called muddled ducks. The hybrid offspring are often fertile, resulting in fewer pure mottled ducks every year. An estimated 7 to 12 percent of mottled ducks show signs of hybridization. This is the greatest threat to the conservation of Florida's mottled ducks.

# NORTHERN PINTAIL *(ANAS ACUTA)*

Breeding male pintails have long, pointed tails. Females and nonbreeding males have shorter tails. All pintails have slender bodies, necks, and wings. They are smaller than mallards.

The male has a chocolate-brown head, neck, and wings. The male also has a narrow white stripe on the head and neck, grayish sides, and a white breast. Females and nonbreeding males have mottled brown and white bodies and plain tan heads. The speculum, or inner wing, which shows in flight, is green on the male and bronze on the female.

**Female**

## NORTHERN PINTAIL POPULATION

The northern pintail breeding population has declined from as many as 10 million in the 1950s to about 2.2 million in 2024. Populations decrease during droughts and increase in wetter years. Declines also result from draining wetlands, changing agricultural land use, and poisoning by lead and pesticides picked up during feeding. However, the northern pintail is not in danger of dying out. Habitats are being protected and restored.

Male

Duckling

## HOW TO SPOT

**Size:** Average wingspan 34 inches (86 cm); 1.1 to 3.3 pounds (0.5 to 1.5 kg)

**North American Range:** Alaska and Canada to Costa Rica and the Caribbean

**Habitat:** Shallow wetlands, lakes, ponds, croplands, grasslands, and shortgrass prairies

**Diet:** Plant matter including aquatic plant seeds; seeds and grains of rice, wheat, corn, and barley; and animal matter such as snails, crustaceans, worms, and aquatic insects

Northern pintails form large groups that can include other species. They take off from the water, flying straight up and moving playfully in the air. They seldom fight, but males jab at other males who threaten them. Their complex mating rituals involve dance-like motions, whistles, and chasing each other in flight.

# NORTHERN SHOVELER

## *(SPATULA CLYPEATA)*

The northern shoveler is a medium-sized duck, smaller than a mallard. Breeding males are boldly colored with green heads, rust-colored sides, and white chests and lower sides. The male's upper wing feathers are blue, and his speculum is green. Both colors are visible in flight. Females and juveniles are mottled brown with powder blue on the wings.

The shoveler has a large spoon- or shovel-shaped bill. The bill is black in the breeding male and orange in the female and juvenile. It is lined with lamellae. As shovelers filter food, they keep their heads down, moving them quickly from side to side. Sometimes groups of shovelers stir up food in the water by swimming in large circles. They rest on land but rarely forage there.

The northern shoveler frequents both freshwater and saltwater habitats. It also likes areas with muddy edges, including polluted and stagnant waters, sewage treatment lagoons, and flooded agricultural fields. These areas have plenty of invertebrates to eat.

Male

### HOW TO SPOT

**Size:** Wingspan 27 to 33 inches (69 to 84 cm); 0.9 to 1.8 pounds (0.4 to 0.8 kg)

**North American Range:** Alaska and Canada to Costa Rica and the Caribbean

**Habitat:** Shallow wetlands, coastal marshes, flooded rice fields, lakes, sewage lagoons, and nearby grassy areas

**Diet:** Seeds and aquatic invertebrates, especially crustaceans

**FUN FACT**
Waterfowl can see almost everything in front of, behind, above, and below them all at once because their eyes are on the sides of their head.

Male

Female and duckling

Eclipse (nonbreeding) male

# WOOD DUCK *(AIX SPONSA)*

The beautiful wood duck is one of North America's most recognizable ducks. It is medium sized, larger than a crow and smaller than a goose. Its boxy head has a noticeable crest. The breeding male's color pattern is bold and brilliant. Its eyes are red, and its bill is red with a yellow patch near the base. The head and crest are shiny purplish green. The face and neck are black with white stripes. The back and tail are black, the breast is chestnut red, and the sides are buffy yellow.

## WATERFOWL COLORS

Pigments, including melanins and lipochromes, produce the colors of waterfowl feathers. The colors these pigments produce include black, brown, red, yellow, green, and violet. When combined with certain feather structures, feathers can look blue or iridescent. Iridescence is when the feathers change color depending on the angle of the light hitting them.

After breeding season, males lose their bright coloration. Females and juveniles are mottled grayish brown, with their sides lighter than their backs. Their heads are gray with white rings around their eyes.

Wood ducks stay in small groups of 20 or fewer, avoiding other species. They nest in tree cavities. Nests are as much as 60 feet (18 m) above the ground.

## HOW TO SPOT

**Size:** Wingspan 26 to 29 inches (66 to 73 cm); 1.1 to 2 pounds (0.5 to 0.9 kg)

**North American Range:** Southern Canada to Mexico and the Caribbean

**Habitat:** Swamps, freshwater marshes, streams, beaver ponds, and wet areas with trees

**Diet:** Aquatic plants such as smartweed, water primrose, duckweed, and waterlily; land plants such as acorns, soybeans, millet, wild cherries, and blackberries; and animal matter such as flies, beetles, caterpillars, and snails

Duckling leaving its tree nest

Male

# BARROW'S GOLDENEYE

## *(BUCEPHALA ISLANDICA)*

The Barrow's goldeneye is a small, stocky duck. Its bill is dark and relatively small. Its forehead is steep compared to the common goldeneye. The head is black and iridescent purple. It has a white, teardrop-shaped spot behind the bill and bright yellowish-gold eyes. The back and wings have a black and white pattern; the underside is pure white. Females have grayish bodies and russet-colored heads. Their bills are yellowish.

### HOW TO SPOT

**Size:** Wingspan 28 to 29 inches (70 to 73 cm); 1.3 to 2.9 pounds (0.6 to 1.3 kg)

**North American Range:** Alaska, western Canada, western United States, eastern Canada, and Maine

**Habitat:** Rocky marine coasts and shallow freshwater bodies, including lakes and ponds in northern mountains and forested areas

**Diet:** Insect larvae such as damselflies, dragonflies, and mayflies; crayfish and small crustaceans; some aquatic vegetation; mollusks such as blue mussels and periwinkles; and small fish

Male

Female

Female with ducklings

**FUN FACT**

Barrow's goldeneyes often lay eggs in nest boxes. People can set up nest boxes for these ducks in late winter, long before breeding season.

Male

Ninety percent of Barrow's goldeneyes breed and winter west of the Rocky Mountains. They spend most of their time on the water, resting or diving for invertebrates. These ducks' wings often make a whistling sound during flight.

These ducks are cavity nesters. They sometimes reuse cavities from previous years. They prefer cavities in dead trees near the water, up to 48 feet (15 m) above ground.

# BUFFLEHEAD *(BUCEPHALA ALBEOLA)*

The tiny bufflehead has a large, round head. Its bill is short and bluish gray. The breeding male is black on top and white on the sides and underside. Its black head appears iridescent green and purple up close and has a large white patch that wraps around the back.

Females and juveniles are grayish brown with light gray fronts and undersides and small white patches on the cheeks. Adult males have large white wing patches visible during flight. These patches are smaller in females and juveniles. Both sexes have dark eyes.

**FUN FACT**

The word *buffle* once meant "buffalo." Early observers apparently saw a likeness between the duck's head and the bison, which settlers called buffalo.

Male

Female

Buffleheads form pairs or small groups but not flocks. They are energetic birds and fast fliers. Bufflehead pairs stay together for several years. They show complex courtship behavior throughout the year. This helps form and maintain pairs. They are cavity nesters, often using the small cavities made by a species of woodpecker called the northern flicker.

## HOW TO SPOT

**Size:** Average wingspan 22 inches (55 cm); 0.7 to 1.3 pounds (0.3 to 0.6 kg)

**North American Range:** Alaska and Canada through Mexico

**Habitat:** Northern lakes and southern coasts with shallow bays

**Diet:** In fresh water: insect larvae, small crustaceans, snails, clams, and some aquatic plants; in salt water: shrimp, crabs, small crustaceans, snails, mussels, fish eggs, and fish

Male

Ducklings

# CANVASBACK *(AYTHYA VALISINERIA)*

Canvasbacks are large ducks with thick necks. They have large heads that slope down to their dark bills. They hold their heads high in the water. Their short tails slope down toward the water.

The breeding male canvasback's head and neck are bright rusty red. His breast and tail are black, and his body is white. During the nonbreeding season, he becomes shades of light brown with black and rusty-red markings. The female is lighter brown, and her body is light gray rather than white. Male canvasbacks have red eyes. Females have dark eyes.

Female

## HOW TO SPOT

**Size:** Wingspan 31 to 35 inches (79 to 89 cm); 2 to 3.5 pounds (0.9 to 1.6 kg)

**North American Range:** Alaska, central Canada, United States, and Mexico

**Habitat:** Lakes, deep marshes, bays, ponds, and coastal waters

**Diet:** A variety of both plant and animal material

Male

## FUN FACT

The canvasback's scientific name, *Aythya valisineria*, is a nod to its favorite food, aquatic wild celery, whose genus name is *Vallisneria*. Canvasbacks eat so much of this plant that their meat tastes like celery.

Male

Female with ducklings

Canvasbacks are divers with strong webbed feet. They can dive up to 30 feet (9 m). They open their bills under mud to dig out roots. During the nonbreeding season, canvasbacks gather on the water in huge groups called rafts. A raft may have thousands to tens of thousands of individuals, often including other divers such as redheads and scaups. Canvasbacks rarely venture onto dry land, sleeping on the water with bills tucked under their wings.

# COMMON GOLDENEYE

## *(BUCEPHALA CLANGULA)*

The common goldeneye is medium sized with a large, triangular head and short tail. It is named for its bright yellowish-gold eyes, present in both sexes. The male's iridescent-green head often appears black. He has a black neck, back, and tail with white sides and a large round white spot below each eye. The female has a chocolate-brown head and gray body. Her bill is black with a yellow tip. Both sexes display white patches on their wings during flight.

Common goldeneyes are fast fliers. Their wings make a whistling sound with every wingbeat. These birds dive in waters up to 20 feet (6 m) deep, flocking together and diving at the same time. They are strong underwater swimmers and rarely walk on land. Compared to most ducks, common goldeneyes are aggressive and often outcompete other species in defense of nesting or foraging territories.

Female

**FUN FACT**

The beating wings of goldeneyes produce a whistling sound that can be heard 0.5 miles (0.8 km) away. These ducks can be heard before they are seen.

Male preening

Female with ducklings

## HOW TO SPOT

**Size:** Wingspan 30 to 33 inches (77 to 83 cm); 1.3 to 2.9 pounds (0.6 to 1.3 kg)

**North American Range:** Alaska, Canada, United States, and into northern Mexico

**Habitat:** Northern boreal forests, coastal waters, and inland lakes

**Diet:** Aquatic invertebrates including crabs, shrimp, crayfish, small crustaceans, mussels, aquatic insects and larvae; fish and fish eggs; and aquatic vegetation such as seeds and tubers

# COMMON MERGANSER

## *(MERGUS MERGANSER)*

Common mergansers are long, slender ducks, slightly larger than mallards. Their wings are thin and pointed, and their bills are straight, narrow, and serrated, or jagged. Adult males have mostly white bodies, black backs, and iridescent-greenish heads. Females have grayish-brown bodies, whitish chins and breasts, and rusty-red heads with shaggy crests on the back. Both sexes have red bills.

Male

## HOW TO SPOT

**Size:** Average wingspan 34 inches (86 cm); 2 to 4.9 pounds (0.9 to 2.2 kg)

**North American Range:** Alaska and most of Canada, most of the United States except the southeast, and north-central Mexico

**Habitat:** Rivers, lakes, and saltwater estuaries

**Diet:** Fish; aquatic invertebrates such as insects, mollusks, crustaceans, and worms; frogs; small mammals and birds; and plants

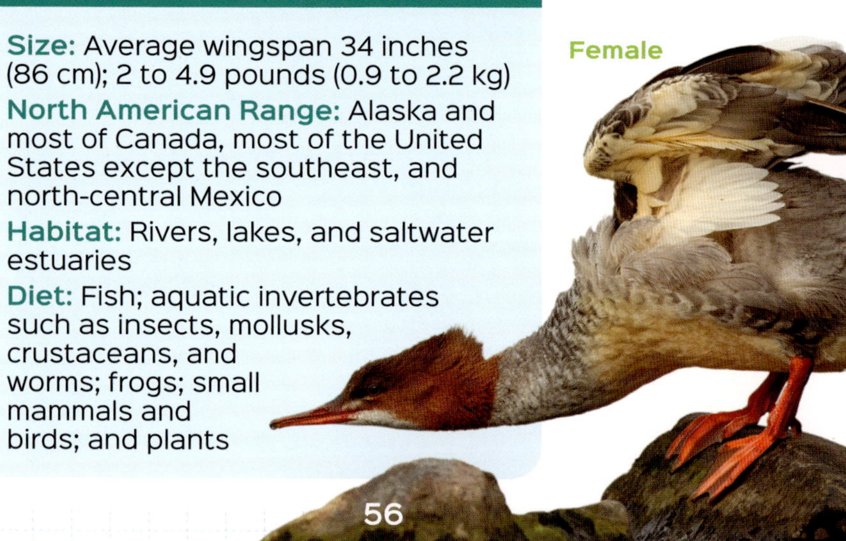

Female

Common mergansers nest near water in large tree cavities, rock crevices, or holes under tree bark. Within a day or two of hatching, the young leap from the nest cavity to the forest floor. Young can feed on their own shortly after hatching. They feed at the water's surface for the first three days after hatching; by eight days old, they are excellent divers. When feeding, adult common mergansers often dive together. They can stay underwater for as long as two minutes, but most dives last less than 30 seconds.

**FUN FACT**

**The common merganser controls the population of fish such as bass and perch in lakes and ponds. This helps the fish thrive rather than overpopulating and using up all the resources.**

Female

Ducklings

# GREATER SCAUP *(AYTHYA MARILA)*

The breeding male greater scaup has a rounded head. It has a black head, neck, and tail. Its white body has thin black bars on the back. It has a bluish bill and yellow eyes. Its head is iridescent green. The female is solid brown with a darker brown head and a white patch above the bill. The nonbreeding male shows a mixture of male and female characteristics and is overall mottled brown.

Female

Male

**FUN FACT**

In winter, coastal bays contain greater scaup flocks of thousands of birds. Most of the birds face into the water's current, or flow.

Greater scaup can dive up to 23 feet (7 m). However, they usually dive in waters of 7 feet (2 m) or less, digging up invertebrates from a lake or ocean floor. The ducks feed by sticking their bills in the mud, then opening and closing them while swimming forward.

## HOW TO SPOT

**Size:** Wingspan 28 to 31 inches (72 to 79 cm); 1.5 to 3 pounds (0.7 to 1.4 kg)

**North American Range:** Alaska and Canada to western Mexico and north-central and eastern United States

**Habitat:** Tundra wetlands, shallow lakes and ponds, coasts, and reservoirs

**Diet:** Aquatic invertebrates such as mollusks, insects, and crustaceans; some aquatic plants and seeds

Duckling

Male

# HOODED MERGANSER

## *(LOPHODYTES CUCULLATUS)*

Hooded mergansers are crow-sized ducks with thin, serrated bills for catching fish. They have thin wings and long, rounded tails. The hooded merganser has a fan-shaped hood, or crest, which makes its head look huge. Raising or lowering the crest changes the head shape.

The breeding male has a black and white striped back and breast, rusty-brown sides, and bright yellow eyes. A large white patch is on the sides of the hood. Females and juveniles have grayish-brown bodies, rusty-brown crests, and dark eyes.

Male

### HOW TO SPOT

**Size:** Wingspan 24 to 26 inches (60 to 66 cm); 1.1 to 2 pounds (0.5 to 0.9 kg)

**North American Range:** Southern Canada into the United States

**Habitat:** Freshwater lakes, ponds, streams, and rivers; marshes; and protected bays

**Diet:** Small fish, aquatic insects, crayfish, mollusks, amphibians, and some vegetation

Female with crayfish

The hooded merganser feeds by sight. Its eyesight is equally good above and below the water. Ducklings can make shallow dives for food at only one day old.

The male courts females by expanding his hood and giving a deep, groaning, frog-like call. These ducks nest in tree cavities 10 to 50 feet (3 to 15 m) above the ground. They also nest readily in boxes.

Duckling

## HIGH NESTS

Canada geese and several duck species, including hooded mergansers, wood ducks, Barrow's goldeneyes, and black-bellied whistling ducks, nest in trees. On the Greenland coast, barnacle geese nest on high cliffs. Tree and cliff nests protect birds from land predators. When ducklings or goslings hatch, they jump from the cliff or nest to the ground or water below. Their light, down-covered bodies absorb the impact, usually preventing injury during landing.

# LESSER SCAUP *(AYTHYA AFFINIS)*

The lesser scaup, sometimes called the bluebill, is a crow-sized diving duck. Feathers form a small peak on the head. The back of the head and neck are flat. The head, breast, and rear of breeding males are glossy black. The back is gray, and the sides are white. The head appears iridescent purplish. Both sexes have light blue bills.

Females are a rich chocolate brown. This coloring is darker on the head, breast, and tail and lighter on the sides and wings. Most have white patches behind their bills. Nonbreeding males show characteristics of both females and breeding males.

**Male**

**Female**

Migrating and wintering lesser scaup gather in rafts of hundreds or thousands on large lakes, coastal bays, and wetlands. They are often the only species present. Greater scaup may be found in the same area, but the two species rarely intermix. These winter habitats contain important food sources such as small mussels and clams. Due to climate change and exploding populations of zebra mussels, which are a food source, lesser scaup now winter more frequently on the Great Lakes.

Male

## HOW TO SPOT

**Size:** Wingspan 27 to 31 inches (68 to 78 cm); 1.1 to 2.4 pounds (0.5 to 1.1 kg)

**North American Range:** Central Alaska and western, central, and southern Canada to Panama and the Caribbean

**Habitat:** Large lakes and reservoirs, coastal bays and estuaries, and marshes

**Diet:** Mostly aquatic invertebrates including mollusks, insects, and crustaceans; some aquatic plants and seeds

Adult female with ducklings

# RED-BREASTED MERGANSER

## *(MERGUS SERRATOR)*

The red-breasted merganser, or sawbill, has a long, thin, serrated bill that helps with catching fish. The bird is crow sized. The breeding male has a dark green head with a shaggy crest, a white neck band, a cinnamon-red breast, and red eyes. The back is greenish black bordered by white, and the sides are gray. Females and nonbreeding males have grayish-brown bodies with white wing bars. Their breasts are whitish with gray spots, and their heads are rusty-brown. Both sexes have reddish-orange bills with black tips and reddish-orange legs.

The feet of red-breasted mergansers are far back on their bodies, so they do not walk well. To fly, they must run across the water. These ducks dive for fish. Each dive lasts up to 44 seconds and can reach 30 feet (9 m) in depth. Red-breasted mergansers herd schools of small fish to the surface. Other birds wait at the surface to feed on the fish.

### HOW TO SPOT

**Size:** Wingspan 26 to 29 inches (66 to 74 cm); 1.8 to 3 pounds (0.8 to 1.4 kg)

**North American Range:** Alaska, Canada, southern Greenland, and throughout the United States into northwestern Mexico

**Habitat:** Sheltered saltwater estuaries and bays, boreal forest wetlands of both fresh and salt water, oceans, lakes, and rivers

**Diet:** Small fish, crustaceans, insects, and tadpoles

Male, *left*, and female, *right*

Courtship display

Ducklings

Male

## WATERFOWL FLYING SPEEDS

The average waterfowl flying speed is about 50 miles per hour (80 kmh). Blue-winged and green-winged teals are among the slowest fliers, averaging about 30 miles per hour (48 kmh). Mallards with a 50-mile-per-hour (80 kmh) tailwind have traveled 800 miles (1,290 km) in eight hours, an average speed of 100 miles per hour (160 kmh). A red-breasted merganser being followed by an airplane also reached a flying speed of 100 miles per hour (160 kmh). This is the current speed record for a waterfowl.

# REDHEAD *(AYTHYA AMERICANA)*

Redheads are slightly smaller than canvasbacks, with rounded heads and steep foreheads. Male redheads have bright cinnamon-red heads, black breasts and tails, and light gray bodies. Their eyes are yellow. Females' bodies are light brown. They have dark eyes. Both males and females have gray bills with black tips.

**Female, *left*, and male, *right***

## NEST PARASITISM

Some waterfowl species lay their eggs in the nests of other females of the same or different species. The foster mothers raise the ducklings as their own. This strategy is known as nest parasitism or egg dumping. Waterfowl known to do this include redheads, canvasbacks, wood ducks, ruddy ducks, hooded mergansers, and snow geese. In one study, more than 90 percent of canvasback nests contained redhead eggs.

## HOW TO SPOT

**Size:** Wingspan 30 to 31 inches (75 to 79 cm); 1.3 to 3.3 pounds (0.6 to 1.5 kg)

**North American Range:** Central Alaska, southern Canada, and the United States to Guatemala and the Caribbean

**Habitat:** Wetlands, especially Midwestern prairie potholes; the Great Lakes; the Gulf Coast; and other coastlines

**Diet:** Submerged aquatic organisms including algae, bulrush, pondweed, widgeon grass, fish eggs, snails, zebra mussels, and aquatic insects

Male

Female with ducklings

Redheads and canvasbacks are often found together during both the breeding and wintering seasons. Outside the breeding season, redheads gather in huge rafts on the water, often mixing with canvasbacks, scaups, wigeons, and coots. They dive in shallower water than most diving ducks and often get food in the same way as dabbling ducks, by tipping up in the water. Redheads practice nest parasitism.

# RING-NECKED DUCK

## *(AYTHYA COLLARIS)*

The ring-necked duck has a large head and thin neck. This duck has a peaked head that flattens when it dives. It is named for the thin chestnut-brown ring on the male's black neck. The duck's bill is gray with a broad white ring just above the black tip.

Female

Male

## HOW TO SPOT

**Size:** Wingspan 24 to 25 inches (62 to 63 cm); 1.1 to 2 pounds (0.5 to 0.9 kg)

**North American Range:** Central Alaska, central and southern Canada, United States, Mexico, Nicaragua to Panama, and the Caribbean

**Habitat:** Shallow freshwater bodies; wetlands including marshes, beaver ponds, cattle ponds, and flooded agricultural fields

**Diet:** Leaves, stems, seeds, and tubers of submerged plants such as pondweed, water lilies, wild celery, and wild rice; aquatic invertebrates such as clams, snails, insect larvae, midges, earthworms, and leeches

The male has a black head, back, and tail and light gray sides with a whitish mark on the chest. The female's body and the top of her head are solid brown. Her face is gray. She has a white patch around the base of her bill and a white ring around both eyes. Her bill is like the male's.

Ring-necked ducks are silent except during mating displays. Then, males produce a whistling sound. Females produce a softer, rolling *trrr* sound. Unlike most diving ducks, ring-necked ducks can take off directly from the water without a running start. They migrate late in fall and early in spring and form huge flocks during migration.

Ducklings

Male

# RUDDY DUCK *(OXYURA JAMAICENSIS)*

Ruddy ducks are between a robin and a crow in size. Their necks are short and thick. They have compact bodies and stiff, spiky tails, which they hold upright. Their bills are broad like a spatula.

During breeding season, the male is boldly colored. He has a black cap, white cheeks, and a rusty-red body. The tops of the wings are dark, and his bill is bright blue. In winter, his body fades to a dull grayish brown. The bill turns from blue to gray, like the female's. Females and juveniles are a similar grayish brown. They have light cheek patches with a blurry stripe across them.

**FUN FACT**

**Ruddy ducks avoid predators by sinking beneath the water's surface. They also build camouflaged nests in thick vegetation.**

Male

## HOW TO SPOT

**Size:** Wingspan 22 to 24 inches (56 to 62 cm); 0.7 to 2 pounds (0.3 to 0.9 kg)

**North American Range:** Western Alaska, southern Canada, United States to Honduras, and the Caribbean

**Habitat:** Marshes, lakes, rivers, ponds, and coastal estuaries

**Diet:** Zooplankton, aquatic insects, and other invertebrates such as shrimp and snails; some plant material such as pondweed, arrowhead, water lilies, and duckweed

Male

Female with duckling

The ruddy duck does not move well on land. Winter flocks sometimes mix with coots but seldom with other ducks. During the breeding season, ruddy ducks are aggressive toward their own and other species.

# BLACK SCOTER

### *(MELANITTA AMERICANA)*

Black scoters are medium sized and have rounded heads and short bills and tails. The male has a sleek, velvety black body and a black bill with a large yellow knob at the base. Females and juveniles are mottled dark brown with solid dark brown head caps and paler cheeks. Black scoters keep the same plumage throughout the year.

Male

## HOW TO SPOT

**Size:** Wingspan 27.6 to 28.3 inches (70 to 72 cm); males 2 to 2.4 pounds (0.9 to 1.1 kg), female weight unavailable

**North American Range:** West Coast from Alaska to California, eastern Canada, Great Lakes region and far northeastern United States, and along the US East and Gulf Coasts

**Habitat:** Northern forest lakes, inland lakes and large rivers, and ocean coastlines

**Diet:** Aquatic insects and larvae, small mollusks and crustaceans, fish eggs, plant material such as iris and pondweed, shellfish such as mussels and clams, and some marine worms

In the far north, this species often rests on the water in the open sea. It can be identified by its frequent mellow whistling calls. Its wings make a whistling sound in flight. During winter, it gathers in flocks of tens of thousands along both the Pacific and Atlantic coastlines.

Black scoter numbers are declining significantly in their wintering area on Puget Sound in Washington. Increasing development has damaged and polluted the ducks' foraging areas. Nearshore fish farming also reduces their habitat.

Male

Female

# COMMON EIDER

## *(SOMATERIA MOLLISSIMA)*

Eiders are restricted to the farthest northern seacoasts around the world. The common eider is the Northern Hemisphere's largest duck. It has a heavy body and a long, sloping bill that extends nearly to the crown of the head. The breeding male is white on top with a black breast, belly, sides, and tail. It has a black cap on the head and a round white spot in front of the tail. The nape of the neck and cheeks are pale green. The bill is green to yellowish orange. The female is rusty brown with dark brown lines along the back, breast, and sides.

**FUN FACT**

**People gather eider down from empty nests of the common eider. Eider down is extremely lightweight and highly insulating. It is the finest type of down.**

Male

Female

## HOW TO SPOT

**Size:** Wingspan 37 to 39 inches (95 to 98 cm); 2.9 to 5.7 pounds (1.3 to 2.6 kg)

**North American Range:** Coastal areas of Alaska, Canada, southern Greenland, and northeastern United States

**Habitat:** Marine coasts near rocky coastlines, tundra and taiga in the far north, and small islands

**Diet:** Marine invertebrates, mostly mollusks, crustaceans, and marine worms; fish eggs

Female with ducklings

Common eiders nest in the far north near rocky shores or on islands. They hide their nests in tall grass and remain still for weeks during incubation. Some nest individually, but they often form nesting colonies. Ducklings form groups of up to 150, and the ducklings remain together as they mature. In winter, common eiders form flocks of thousands.

# HARLEQUIN DUCK

## *(HISTRIONICUS HISTRIONICUS)*

The harlequin duck is crow sized, with a large head and steeply sloping forehead. The male's body is mostly slate blue with rusty-red sides and head patches. It has white stripes on the back and sides. There are several white spots and a large white crescent on the head. The female's body is grayish brown all over. It has white around the bill and eyes and a white spot on the cheeks. Both sexes have small bluish-gray bills and grayish legs.

### HOW TO SPOT

**Size:** Wingspan 22 to 26 inches (56 to 66 cm); 1.1 to 1.8 pounds (0.5 to 0.8 kg)

**North American Range:** Alaska, western Canada, southern Greenland, and northeastern United States

**Habitat:** Near rocky shores with strong winds and big waves

**Diet:** Aquatic insects and fish eggs; tidal invertebrates including crabs, barnacles, and mussels; snails; and insects

Female

Male

During the breeding season, harlequin ducks often feed by skimming invertebrates off the water's surface. They spend considerable time foraging underwater, often in strong currents. They are excellent swimmers, diving as deep as 70 feet (21 m) for as long as 45 seconds.

Harlequin ducks are monogamous. They maintain pair bonds for years. Females seek out their mates after returning to their molting and wintering grounds.

Female with ducklings

Male

**FUN FACT**

Harlequin ducks live in spots with challenging conditions, including rushing rivers and rough coastal surf. They climb on steep, slippery rocks, and adults often show evidence of broken bones.

# KING EIDER *(SOMATERIA SPECTABILIS)*

The king eider is a large, heavyset duck with a short, heavy bill. Behind the breeding male's red bill is a large, rounded, bulging plate that is orange with a black rim. The top of the head is pale blue, and the cheeks are pale green. The female lacks the bulging plate.

The male's body is black and white. Long black scapular feathers, located at the base of the wing, look like a pair of vertical sails on the duck's back. The female is mostly rusty brown with a marbling of dark brown and black on the sides and breast. The female's bill is black.

When foraging in seabeds for marine invertebrates, king eiders dive as deep as 85 feet (26 m). In shallow lakes, they tip up to strain prey from surface waters. King eiders forage and migrate in flocks that often include other sea ducks.

Male

Juvenile male

Female

## HOW TO SPOT

**Size:** Wingspan 35 to 40 inches (89 to 102 cm); 2.6 to 4.6 pounds (1.2 to 2.1 kg)

**North American Range:** Coastal regions along Alaska, Canada, Greenland, and northeastern United States

**Habitat:** Near ocean coasts or interior lakes in high tundra, fjords, open ocean, rocky coasts at southern edge of sea ice, and Hudson Bay

**Diet:** Shellfish, crustaceans, algae, insects, echinoderms such as sea stars, and plant matter including eelgrass, widgeon grass, and sedges

Male

# LONG-TAILED DUCK

## *(CLANGULA HYEMALIS)*

The long-tailed duck is named for the two very long black tail feathers worn by the male for most of the year. The species is small and slender with a small bill and gray legs and feet. These birds are most often seen during the winter. The winter male has a white head with a large black patch and tan cheeks. The breast is white with a broad black band. The body, wings, and tail are black, and the back is black with white plumes. The short bill is black with a pink band.

### HOW TO SPOT

**Size:** Wingspan 28 to 28.3 inches (71 to 72 cm); 1.1 to 2.4 pounds (0.5 to 1.1 kg)

**North American Range:** Alaska, coastal Canada, coastal Greenland, Washington, and northeastern United States

**Habitat:** Arctic tundra wetlands, large lakes, coasts, and open ocean

**Diet:** Small aquatic invertebrates including insects and crustaceans, fish eggs, plant matter, mussels, fish, and zooplankton

**Nonbreeding male**

Female with ducklings

**FUN FACT**
The long-tailed duck is an excellent diver. Some long-tailed ducks have been caught in fishing nets at a depth of 240 feet (73 m) off Wolfe Island in Lake Ontario.

Nonbreeding female

The summer male's head, neck, and body are dark, and it has a white face patch. Females and juveniles have mottled brown bodies, brown heads and cheeks, and white faces.

Long-tailed ducks are expert divers. They dive deep to feed. While foraging, they spend three to four times as much time underwater as on the surface—more than any other diving duck.

# SPECTACLED EIDER

### *(SOMATERIA FISCHERI)*

The spectacled eider is large with a short, thick neck and a heavy body. The bill is thick, with feathers extending down to the nostrils. Males' bills are bright orange, and females' bills are bluish gray.

The breeding male's back is white, and the breast, sides, underside, tail, and flight feathers are black. The duck's head is olive and brown with a large pair of white spectacles rimmed in black surrounding the eyes. The female and juvenile are rich brown throughout the year, mottled with darker brown. Their spectacles are lighter brown. Outside the breeding season, males are colored like females.

During the breeding season, spectacled eiders act like dabblers. They feed on shallow-water vegetation and small invertebrates. In winter, they may dive as deep as 250 feet (76 m) to feed.

**FUN FACT**

**After attaching satellite transmitters to some spectacled eiders in the 1990s, the US Fish and Wildlife Service discovered that the birds winter in the open sea between Alaska and Russia and north of Alaska.**

Female with ducklings

Male

## HOW TO SPOT

**Size:** Average wingspan 33 inches (84 cm); 2.9 to 4 pounds (1.3 to 1.8 kg)

**North American Range:** Alaska

**Habitat:** Coastal marshes, tundra, lakes, river mouths, small islands in ponds, and the Bering Sea

**Diet:** Insects, seeds, plants, and aquatic invertebrates, especially mollusks, marine worms, and crabs

Male

Female

# STELLER'S EIDER

## *(POLYSTICTA STELLERI)*

Steller's eiders are the smallest of the four eider species. They are crow sized. An adult male Steller's eider has a white head with black eye spots. It has a moss-green patch on the back of the head and another in front of the eyes. The throat, neck, back, and tail are black. The wings are black with broad white edges. The secondary feathers, which are the lower feathers of the section of wing near the body, are blue with a white edge. The breast is buffy orange with a circular black spot on the side. Female Steller's eiders are mottled dark brown to cinnamon with light eye rings. Juveniles look similar but are lighter brown. Both sexes have bluish-gray bills, legs, and feet.

### HOW TO SPOT

**Size:** Wingspan 28 to 30 inches (70 to 76 cm); 1.5 to 2.2 pounds (0.7 to 1 kg)

**North American Range:** Alaska

**Habitat:** Small ponds in coastal tundra sedge marshes and in coastal lagoons and bays

**Diet:** Aquatic insect larvae, small crustaceans such as fairy and tadpole shrimp, aquatic plant seeds, mollusks, and marine worms

Male

Female

During breeding season, Steller's eiders feed like dabbling ducks on plant material and invertebrates near the water's surface. During molting and wintering, they feed by diving or foraging in eelgrass or seaweed beds. In deeper water, they dive to find invertebrates to eat. Often, flocks form a long line and dive together.

Males and females

Male

# SURF SCOTER

## *(MELANITTA PERSPICILLATA)*

Unlike other scoters, surf scoters breed only in North America, specifically in Alaska and northwestern Canada. The surf scoter has a large head, thick neck, and broad bill. Males are mostly shiny black with large white patches on their heads and necks. They are easily identified by their large, rounded bills, which are black, orange, and white. Females are dark brown and usually have two white face patches. Juveniles are similar but lighter brown.

Female

**FUN FACT**

The surf scoter has special salt glands that filter salt from seawater and prey. The glands concentrate salt from the bird's blood. The salt is then released from the nostrils.

Male

## HOW TO SPOT

**Size:** Wingspan 29.9 to 30.3 inches (76 to 77 cm); 2 to 2.9 pounds (0.9 to 1.3 kg)

**North American Range:** West Coast from Alaska to Mexico's Baja California; interior of Alaska, Canada, and northeastern United States; and along the US East and Gulf Coasts

**Habitat:** Forests and tundra, ocean coasts, bays, estuaries, and inland lakes in the far north

**Diet:** Freshwater invertebrates such as insects, freshwater plant material, marine plant material, herring spawn, and marine invertebrates such as mussels, clams, snails, crabs, and marine worms

Male

Like other sea birds, surf scoters travel in large flocks after breeding. They go to specific coastal locations where they molt and replace their flying feathers before moving to winter locations. At winter locations, they dive to forage for mussels and clams.

Male

# WHITE-WINGED SCOTER

## *(MELANITTA DEGLANDI)*

The white-winged scoter is the largest of the scoters. Unlike the other two scoter species, it has large white wing patches that are visible both in flight and at rest. The adult male is solid silky black with a small, white, teardrop-shaped mark around each eye. Its bill is orange with a large, black, feather-covered bulge at the base. Females and juveniles are brown. They have two circular white splotches on their faces.

Female

## HOW TO SPOT

**Size:** Average wingspan 31 inches (80 cm); 2.2 to 4 pounds (1 to 1.8 kg)

**North American Range:** Along the West Coast from Alaska to Mexico's Baja California, Canada, the Great Lakes and northeastern United States, and along the US East and Gulf Coasts

**Habitat:** Far northern forests or tundra near shallow freshwater lakes, seacoasts, and large lakes

**Diet:** Freshwater crustaceans, insects, aquatic plant matter, and mollusks including clams, oysters, periwinkles, mussels, and scallops

These ducks gather in large flocks over the sea, flying low in long, wavering lines. When migrating, they fly much higher, and the flocks are much smaller. Sometimes an entire flock suddenly drops hundreds of feet, making a loud rushing noise.

Their diving habits change depending on location. Along the coasts and at sea, white-winged scoters dive for marine invertebrates. On dives, they use their bills to rip shellfish from the rocks. In fresh water during breeding season, they feed mostly on surface organisms.

Male

Juvenile male

# BRANT *(BRANTA BERNICLA)*

The brant is a small goose, larger than a mallard and smaller than a Canada goose. Its head, neck, and breast are black. The neck has white markings that form a necklace, which is larger on the male. The wings and back are brown, and the underside is lighter, from pale brown to black. The undertail is white. This goose has large wings and is a strong flier.

The brant is compact, with a shorter neck than most geese. There are two subspecies of brant. The Atlantic brant has a lighter brown and white belly. The much darker black brant is found on the West Coast.

Brant breed in the tundra, farther north than any other species of goose, and they migrate farther than most geese. During migration, their flocks fly thousands of feet high over open ocean. They are the fastest and strongest geese during flight.

**FUN FACT**

**Black brant migrate nonstop for 3,000 miles (4,830 km) from coastal Alaska to Mexico, where they overwinter. While making this journey in 60 to 72 hours, they lose half their body weight.**

Female

Juvenile male

Male

## HOW TO SPOT

**Size:** Wingspan 41 to 43 inches (105 to 108 cm); 2.2 to 3.7 pounds (1 to 1.7 kg)

**North American Range:** West Coast from Alaska to Mexico's Baja California, coastal areas of Canada and Greenland, and northeastern United States

**Habitat:** Arctic tundra, marshes, islands, lagoons, estuaries, salt marshes, mudflats, sandspits, and ocean shores

**Diet:** Aquatic life such as pondweed, arrow grass, mosses, eelgrass, and large green algae; hair grass; alkali grass; cultivated grasses; saxifrage; sedges; and saltmarsh grasses

# CACKLING GOOSE

## *(BRANTA HUTCHINSII)*

The cackling goose looks very similar to the Canada goose. But cackling geese are smaller, only slightly larger than mallards. Their necks are shorter than the necks of Canada geese. The birds are more delicate and have shorter bills. Cackling geese make a higher-pitched sound than the honk of the Canada goose. Also, Canada geese breed throughout the continent, while cackling geese breed in the tundra.

### HOW TO SPOT

**Size:** Wingspan 43 to 44 inches (108 to 111 cm); 3 to 5.3 pounds (1.4 to 2.4 kg)

**North American Range:** Alaska along the West Coast to California, northern and central Canada, and midwestern and northeastern United States

**Habitat:** Arctic tundra, islands in small lakes or marshes, wetlands, meadows, agricultural fields, lakes, and reservoirs

**Diet:** Sedges, grasses, small flowering plants, seeds, berries, agricultural crops, and grains

### FUN FACT

In 2004, the four smallest subspecies of the Canada goose were moved into their own species, the cackling goose.

The plumage of the cackling goose is similar to that of the Canada goose. It has a black head and neck with a white chin strap. Its body is grayish brown, lighter underneath, with white undertail feathers. Some have white collars separating their black necks from their bodies. There is a sharp angle between the bill and the forehead. The bill, legs, and feet are black.

# CANADA GOOSE *(BRANTA CANADENSIS)*

The Canada goose is one of the most well-known and numerous North American waterfowl. Its large, V-shaped flocks travel north in spring and south in fall. The movement of these birds signals the changing seasons.

There are seven currently recognized subspecies of the Canada goose. In general, smaller subspecies are found farther north and darker subspecies farther west. Both sexes tend to seek out mates who match their size.

## ENERGY-EFFICIENT MIGRATION

Canada geese and other waterfowl often fly in a V formation during migration. This formation is highly energy efficient. Birds rotate in and out of the lead position, which is the most tiring position. This energy-saving method of flight allows Canada geese to fly up to 1,490 miles (2,400 km) during a single day of migration.

The Canada goose has a long black head and neck with a wide white chinstrap. Its back and wings are varying shades of grayish brown to dark brown, fading to a lighter cream color underneath. The undertail is white. The bill, feet, and legs are dark gray to black.

Canada geese tend to mate for life. If one member of the pair dies, the other finds a new mate. Pairs, along with their goslings, often join other families to form a crèche, a group that stays together until the next breeding season.

## HOW TO SPOT

**Size:** Wingspan 50 to 67 inches (127 to 170 cm); 6.6 to 20 pounds (3 to 9 kg)

**North American Range:** Alaska, Canada, United States, and northern Mexico

**Habitat:** Lakes, rivers, ponds, and open, grassy areas including yards, lawns, parks, and agricultural fields

**Diet:** Sedges, skunk cabbage, eelgrass, grains, berries, and grasses including domesticated grasses

# EMPEROR GOOSE *(ANSER CANAGICUS)*

Within North America, the emperor goose is found only in Alaska. It is small and rare. This goose has a short neck and bill. Its body is bluish gray or silver gray with feathers edged in white, and the tail feathers are white. The head and back of the neck are white, and the throat is black. In summer, when this goose feeds in iron-oxide-rich tide pools, its head becomes stained orange. The bill is pink, and the legs are orange.

## HOW TO SPOT

**Size:** Wingspan 48 to 56 inches (122 to 142 cm); average 6.2 pounds (2.8 kg)

**North American Range:** Western and southern Alaskan coasts

**Habitat:** Low tundra grasslands near rivers and tidal habitats such as marshes, mudflats, lagoons, and rocky shores

**Diet:** Mussels, barnacles, clams, shoots and roots of grasses and sedges, berries, eelgrass, and tundra and marsh plants such as marsh arrow grass

Up to 90 percent of the world's emperor goose population nests on the Yukon-Kuskokwim Delta on Alaska's west coast. These geese migrate to and winter in other parts of Alaska. Emperor geese are monogamous. They begin breeding at three years of age. Only about 10 percent of goslings survive their first year.

# GREATER WHITE-FRONTED GOOSE *(ANSER ALBIFRONS)*

The greater white-fronted goose is medium sized, smaller than a Canada goose, and it has a thick neck and short orange legs. It is named for the white band of feathers at the base of its short pinkish-yellow bill. As with all geese, males and females have similar color patterns. An adult is mostly brown, with white around the bill, under the tail, and in a thin line along the sides. It has black barring on the breast. The juvenile is brown or brownish gray all over. It lacks the white feathers on the bill and black bars on the breast.

## TULE GOOSE

The tule goose (*Anser albifrons elgasi*) is a larger, darker subspecies of the greater white-fronted goose. Only about 7,500 individuals of this subspecies exist. They are named for their preference for feeding in marshes containing tule rushes. They breed around Alaska's Cook Inlet and winter in the Sacramento Valley of California. They breed in areas of spruce forest that have wet, open bogs, and they winter in marshes.

White-fronted geese are long-distance migrants. In North America, they follow the Pacific and Central Flyways. During the winter, most live west of the Mississippi River in coastal and freshwater marshes and wet meadows. They fly to feeding areas in open country before dawn and can be identified by their musical honking and wavering flights.

## HOW TO SPOT

**Size:** Wingspan 53 inches (135 cm); 4.4 to 7.3 pounds (2 to 3.3 kg)

**North American Range:** From Alaska to western Mexico and from central Canada and the United States to eastern Mexico

**Habitat:** Lakes, ponds, wetlands, wet meadows, mudflats, and tundra

**Diet:** Vegetation such as sedges, grasses, berries, plant tubers, seeds, grains, and aquatic plants

# ROSS'S GOOSE *(ANSER ROSSII)*

The Ross's goose is white with black wing tips. It is about the size of a mallard. The goose has a small head and a short neck and bill. The bill is pink. This bird can occasionally have a dark body with a white face. Juveniles are grayish white with dark bills.

## HOW TO SPOT

**Size:** Wingspan 44 to 46 inches (113 to 116 cm); 2.2 to 3.5 pounds (1 to 1.6 kg)

**North American Range:** Central Canada to western and central United States and northern Mexico

**Habitat:** Fields, marshes, lakes, reservoirs, and wetlands

**Diet:** Plants including roots of grasses and sedges, birch and sedge shoots, cottongrass, chickweed, clover, bulrush, salt grass, and grains

Dark variety

Ross's geese with snow geese

Ross's geese travel in large flocks with snow geese and hybridize with them. As the climate warms, their breeding ranges overlap more, increasing hybridization. Although this goose is relatively rare, its population is increasing. About 95 percent of the breeding population is located in the Queen Maud Gulf Migratory Bird Sanctuary, which is in Canada's Arctic tundra.

Ross's geese form permanent pair bonds, usually starting in the winter or during spring migration. Males attract females using both vocalizations and displays. The geese remain in colonies during breeding.

# SNOW GOOSE *(ANSER CAERULESCENS)*

The usual morph, or form, of the snow goose is solid white with black wing tips, which are visible only during flight. The bill is pink and curved at the base with a black line often called a grin patch. Occasionally, there are blue morphs, which are dark grayish-blue geese with white heads.

Snow geese breed in the tundra, above the Arctic Circle. This means few people see them from late March through October. In the winter, they migrate and winter mostly in areas along the four major flyways. They often stop at national wildlife refuges.

**FUN FACT**

**Snow geese are excellent walkers and fliers. At only three weeks of age, goslings can walk with their parents up to 50 miles (80 km) from their nest to a better feeding area.**

Blue morph

Juveniles migrate south when they are just six to eight weeks old. They fly in V formations or long, diagonal lines to conserve energy during their long flights. Snow geese form pairs during their second spring migration and mate for life.

## HOW TO SPOT

**Size:** Wingspan 54 inches (138 cm); 3.5 to 7.3 pounds (1.6 to 3.3 kg)

**North American Range:** Alaska, Canada, northwestern Greenland, United States, and northern and eastern Mexico

**Habitat:** Tidal marshes, shallow freshwater wetlands, sedge meadows, and agricultural fields

**Diet:** All parts of plants such as sedges, rushes, grasses, forbs, shrubs, willows, and berries; grains and stems of agricultural crops

White morph juvenile

White morph

# TRUMPETER SWAN

### *(CYGNUS BUCCINATOR)*

Trumpeter swans are the largest waterfowl species in North America, reaching more than 6 feet (1.8 m) long from bill to tail. Males are among the world's heaviest flying birds. This swan's long neck remains straight while flying and swimming.

## HOW TO SPOT

**Size:** Wingspan 80 inches (203 cm); 17 to 29 pounds (7.7 to 13 kg)

**North American Range:** Alaska, western and southern Canada, and pockets across the United States

**Habitat:** Open areas near shallow water, ice-free estuaries, lakes, rivers, and agricultural fields

**Diet:** Aquatic life such as pondweed, eelgrass, sedges, rushes, wild rice, and algae; terrestrial plants such as berries, grains, and tubers; small fish and fish eggs; and aquatic insects

Juvenile

The adult is white with a black bill and legs. Juveniles are grayish brown. This swan is named for its bugle-like call, which is lower pitched than the call of the tundra swan. The sound is sometimes compared to a French horn.

Trumpeter swans form permanent pair bonds at age two to four. Pairs travel together during migration. Young swans stay with their parents for the first year, learning migration routes and wintering locations.

**FUN FACT**

**Some hummingbirds have fewer than 1,000 feathers, while some swans have more than 25,000. Feathers make up about one-sixth of a bird's weight.**

Adult with cygnets

# TUNDRA SWAN *(CYGNUS COLUMBIANUS)*

Tundra swans are the most numerous North American swans. They are slightly smaller than trumpeter swans. They have a whistling call.

The tundra swan is a very large bird with a long neck. It is white with a black bill and a yellow spot between the base of the bill and the eyes. The legs and feet are black. Juveniles have some gray on the wings, head, and neck.

## FUN FACT

An adult male swan is called a cob. An adult female is a pen, because the central shafts, or quills, of female flight feathers were once used to make quill pens.

## HOW TO SPOT

**Size:** Wingspan 66 inches (168 cm); 8.4 to 24 pounds (3.8 to 11 kg)

**North American Range:** Alaska, Canada, and northern and western United States

**Habitat:** Arctic tundra, coastal waters, estuaries, some inland lakes, and agricultural fields

**Diet:** Aquatic life such as sedges, saltmarsh starwort, alkali grass, pondweed, and algae; grains; corn; soybeans; mollusks; and arthropods

Adult with cygnets

Two subspecies of tundra swans travel from the high Arctic tundra along separate migration routes to the US West and East Coasts. They fly in flocks of up to 100 swans. They make a bugling call as they migrate. Both the eastern and western populations have been increasing.

# GLOSSARY

**camouflage**
The ability to blend in with the surroundings.

**courtship**
The behavior of male birds seeking to attract a mate.

**crustacean**
An aquatic invertebrate with a hard shell and several pairs of segmented legs.

**cultivated**
Planted and grown by people.

**domestic**
Bred to be tame and useful to people.

**emergent**
Rooted in the bottom of a body of water with stems and leaves reaching above the water's surface.

**incubation**
Keeping eggs warm and safe before they hatch.

**invertebrate**
An animal without a spinal column.

**juvenile**
A young or immature individual.

**mollusk**
An invertebrate animal with a hard shell and soft body.

**molt**
To lose and replace the flying feathers.

**organism**
Any living thing.

**pectoral**
Related to the chest, especially the chest muscles, which control the movement of shoulders.

**plumage**
A bird's feathers, especially the outer feathers that show colors and patterns.

**preen**
To groom using the bill.

**reservoir**
An artificial lake where water is stored for later use.

**ritual**
A set of behaviors repeated in a specific order to serve a special purpose.

**tuber**
An underground stem of certain plants, used for nutrient storage and sometimes reproduction.

# TO LEARN MORE

## FURTHER READINGS

Abell, Tracy. *Birds*. Abdo, 2021.

Graf, Mike. *My Awesome Field Guide to North American Birds*. Rockridge, 2021.

Hoare, Ben. *An Anthology of Exquisite Birds*. DK, 2024.

## ONLINE RESOURCES

To learn more about North American waterfowl, please visit **abdobooklinks.com** or scan this QR code. These links are routinely monitored and updated to provide the most current information available.

# PHOTO CREDITS

Cover Photos: Susan Hodgson/Shutterstock Images, front (top left cinnamon teal, upper right female teal, middle left flying, bottom open wings); Shutterstock Images, front (top right black, upper left mallard, middle right hooded merganser); Ryzhkov Serhii/Shutterstock Images, front (upper middle eider); Wilfred Marissen/Shutterstock Images, front (upper right harlequin); Oral Zirek/Shutterstock Images, front (middle left wood duck); John Fader/Shutterstock Images, front (middle swan); Adrian Eugen Ciobaniuc/Shutterstock Images, front (middle right goose); Maciej Olszewski/Shutterstock Images, front (bottom swimming); Doug McLean/Shutterstock Images, back

Interior Photos: Shutterstock Images, 1 (top left), 1 (top right), 1 (middle), 1 (bottom left), 1 (bottom right), 3 (top left), 3 (top right), 3 (middle right), 4 (top), 4 (bottom left), 4 (bottom middle), 4 (bottom right), 5 (top left), 5 (top middle), 5 (top right), 5 (bottom left), 5 (bottom right), 6, 7 (top), 7 (bottom), 9, 10 (top), 11, 12, 13 (top), 15 (top), 15 (bottom), 16 (top), 17, 19 (top), 19 (bottom), 20, 20–21, 22 (top), 22 (bottom), 23 (left), 23 (right), 24 (top), 24 (bottom), 25 (top), 26 (top), 26 (bottom), 27 (top), 27 (bottom), 28, 29 (top), 30, 32, 33 (bottom), 34 (top), 35, 36, 37 (top), 37 (bottom), 40 (bottom), 42, 42–43, 45 (top), 45 (middle), 45 (bottom), 46 (top), 46 (bottom), 47 (bottom), 48 (left), 48 (right), 49 (top), 49 (bottom), 50 (top), 50 (bottom), 51 (top), 51 (bottom), 52, 52–53, 53 (top), 54–55, 55 (bottom), 56, 56–57, 57 (top), 57 (bottom), 58, 59 (top), 59 (bottom), 60, 61 (top), 62 (bottom), 63 (top), 63 (bottom), 64, 65 (top), 65 (middle), 65 (bottom), 67 (top), 67 (bottom), 68, 68–69, 69 (top), 69 (bottom), 70, 71 (bottom), 72, 73 (top), 74 (top), 74 (bottom), 75, 76 (top), 76 (bottom), 77 (top), 77 (bottom), 78 (bottom), 79 (top), 80, 81 (top), 81 (bottom), 83 (bottom), 84, 84–85, 85 (top), 85 (bottom), 86 (top), 86 (bottom), 87 (top), 89 (top), 89 (bottom), 90, 91 (top), 92, 92–93, 93 (bottom), 94 (top), 94 (bottom), 95 (top), 95 (bottom), 96, 97 (top left), 98, 98–99, 99 (top), 99 (bottom), 100, 100–101, 101 (top), 101 (bottom), 102,

102–103, 103 (top), 103 (bottom), 104 (top), 104 (bottom), 105 (top), 106, 112 (left), 112 (middle), 112 (right); Michael J. Cohen, Photographer/Moment/Getty Images, 3 (middle left), 31 (top), 41 (bottom), 78 (top), 107 (top); Jared Lloyd/Moment/Getty Images, 3 (bottom), 106–107; iStockphoto, 5 (bottom middle), 18, 21 (bottom), 33 (top), 44, 53 (bottom), 58–59, 66, 73 (bottom), 79 (bottom); Gary W. Carter/Corbis Documentary/Getty Images, 8 (top); Callum Fraser/Alamy, 8 (bottom); Russell Burden/ Photodisc/Getty Images, 10 (bottom); Thomas & Pat Leeson/ Science Source, 13 (bottom); Red Line Editorial, 14; George Ostertag/Alamy, 16 (bottom); www.glennbartley/NHPA/ Photoshot/Newscom, 21 (top); Nancy Elwood/Naturesportal/ Moment Open/Getty Images, 25 (bottom); Danita Delimont/Gallo Images Roots RF collection/ Getty Images, 29 (bottom); Elizabeth W. Kearley/Moment/ Getty Images, 31 (bottom), 41 (top); H. Soerensen/blickwinkel/ Agami/Alamy, 34 (bottom); Fernando Flores/Flickr, 38 (top); Bill Gorum/Alamy, 38 (bottom); Rick & Nora Bowers/Alamy, 39 (top); Jim Zipp/Science Source, 39 (bottom); Arthur Morris/Corbis Documentary/Getty Images, 40 (top); NHPA/Photoshot/Newscom, 43; Stan Tekiela Author/ Naturalist/Wildlife Photographer/ Moment/Getty Images, 47 (top), 105 (bottom); Damian Kuzdak/ E+/Getty Images, 55 (top); Tammy Wolfe/Alamy, 61 (bottom); Diana Robinson Photography/ Moment/Getty Images, 62 (top); Enrique Aguirre Aves/ The Image Bank/Getty Images, 71 (top); NatPar Collection/ Alamy, 82; Marco Valentini/ Alamy, 83 (top); Tom Applegate/ Moment/Getty Images, 83 (middle); mallardg500/Moment/ Getty Images, 87 (bottom); Emil Vacek/500Px Plus/Getty Images, 88–89; NHPA/Photoshot/Science Source, 91 (bottom); Anthony Mercieca/Science Source, 93 (top); Stephen J. Krasemann/ Science Source, 97 (top right); Shirley Hawkes/NHPA/Photoshot/ Newscom, 97 (bottom); Krys Bailey/Alamy, 107 (bottom)

**ABDOBOOKS.COM**
Published by Abdo Reference, a division of ABDO, PO Box 398166, Minneapolis, Minnesota 55439. 

Printed in China.
102025
012026

Editor: Marie Pearson
Series Designer: Colleen McLaren
Production Designer: Tara Raymo

**LIBRARY OF CONGRESS CONTROL NUMBER: 2025939289**
**PUBLISHER'S CATALOGING-IN-PUBLICATION DATA**
Names: Hand, Carol, author.
Title: Waterfowl / by Carol Hand
Description: Minneapolis, Minnesota: Abdo Reference, 2026 | Series: North American field guides | Includes online resources and index.
Identifiers: ISBN 9781098298968 (lib. bdg.) | ISBN 9798384932765 (ebook)
Subjects: LCSH: Waterfowl--Juvenile literature. | Birds--Juvenile literature. | Aquatic birds--Juvenile literature. | Birds--Behavior--Juvenile literature. | Zoology--Juvenile literature. | Encyclopedias --Juvenile literature.
Classification: DDC 598.4--dc23